# The LOST PARABLES

## of

## JESUS

as remembered by

His Mother

on the Way to Jerusalem

for The Passover

*by*

# Carl Winderl

*Finishing Line Press*
Georgetown, Kentucky

# The LOST PARABLES

## of

## JESUS

as remembered by

His Mother

on the Way to Jerusalem

for The Passover

Copyright © 2024 by Carl Winderl
ISBN 979-8-88838-756-6 First Edition
All rights reserved under International and Pan-American Copyright Conventions. No part of this book may be reproduced in any manner whatsoever without written permission from the publisher, except in the case of brief quotations embodied in critical articles and reviews.

ACKNOWLEDGMENTS

Thanks eversomuch to:

Leah Huete de Maines
Christen Kincaid
Elizabeth Maines McCleavy
Kevin Maines
and the entire FLP team.

I am blessed by all of their efforts on behalf of my poetry and me.



Publisher: Leah Huete de Maines
Editor: Christen Kincaid
Cover Art: Cover Photo—Bronson Pate at baumanphotographers.com
           Cover Sculpture—*The Teacher* by Scott Stearman at scottstearman.com
Author Photo: Marcus Emerson, MarcusEmerson@pointloma.edu

Cover Design: Elizabeth Maines McCleavy


Order online: www.finishinglinepress.com
              also available on amazon.com

Author inquiries and mail orders:
Finishing Line Press
PO Box 1626
Georgetown, Kentucky 40324
USA

# Table of Contents

**A General Prologue**

    in *tres partes*..................................................................................... 1

**upon leaving Galilee**

    on His trail............................................................................................ 9

    on a stony path.................................................................................. 14

    near to the Sea.................................................................................. 18

    in a grove, or..................................................................................... 20

    that I mayest not............................................................................... 22

**when in Samaria**

    not far past the border ..................................................................... 29

    in Samaria......................................................................................... 39

    not all women .................................................................................. 43

    on the Sunday before........................................................................ 52

    with nare a Samaritan ...................................................................... 57

**so nearing Jerusalem**

    and so ............................................................................................... 65

    : and who ......................................................................................... 67

    on Mount Olivet ............................................................................... 71

    those who glean ............................................................................... 74

    after the Procession .......................................................................... 79

**An Epilogue, in Kind**

    And so, 'tis this Is ............................................................................. 83

for Larry Finger

a teacher who taught so much
    more than literature

like Jesus, he taught students

# A General Prologue

**in *tres partes***

did that other forerunner
Julius Caesar, first initialized as
j.c.,
in his own known world then
stake his claim

in Gaul,
sent unto the *Patres Romae*

news of his
kingdom come
to be called, for so

he had the gall
to proclaim

*veni, vidi, vinci*

while My Son
would in some simplex state
in His inaugural

Proclamation of The Kingdom

Come that He

Was, Is, and ever shall Be

Three-in-One; the Triune—whole,
complete, and entire

when He set out
that fateful &
fatefull cruelest of Aprils
on a pilgrimage

to Passover be

as if wending their way
to Canterbury

to visit a
latterday holy, bliss-
ful martyr, instead He and they

through the then known
world of the Province of Judea
di-

vided, into Its three parts:

Galilee, Samaria, & Judea

where through He
must go
to enter Jerusalem, there

He would unite
for time and for all
eternity

His Kingdom to Come

so, from the shores of
the Sea of Galilee

'twas the next Beginning
when the Word
sallied forth, among whom

His disciples, I too

went, seeing Him win

their trust, hope
faith, and charity; as if
the stories He told were tales

to prepare the Way to

their unbelief and too
to their understanding; so
that, some
of those parables He spoke

they'd later
enflesh in their
memoirs, as
if the very gospel, but

the ones they forgot, those
*The Lost Parables*
I all

remember, and share

with His latterday
followers;

they come to know My Son

through these His
revelations, seen

through His Mother's eyes that
others might realize

and be

wise

alike as when He first
spoke them

: a certain man
  in a nearby country
  lived among three,
  side-by-side
  around about him,
  landowners who would

  devour that certain man
  and his land and
  all his children, and all
  his servants, livestock, and even
  yea, all his possessions;

  but that certain man
  avoided them, all three
  when all together they were

no, not ever when all three were one,
as at the village square;

nay, only when they were one
alone, with him

then did he refute
their malign dispute to dyspossess,
him; yea, instead though

he turned around
each one's wrath upon
the other two
saying that their plot to
overtake was

for both the certain man
and
their odd man out;

'twas thus what the certain man spoke
to each man alone, by himself
singly, and 'twas sore believed by each;

for each
easily believed the deviltries of
the other absent pair;

so then the three warred
among themselves and
thus they destroyed each other;
for out of their self-doubt
the certain man
played upon each other's guilt
of evil intent; and singly
one at a time
he overtook his adversaries;

and in the end
won out

for divided they fell
but he
singly united stood still,

victorious over his
duplicitous, yet even his
triplicitous foe;

fallen by divisive distrust
by the one who lived
in equanimity
though once so surrounded by

enmity,
but which he himself crushed

with dignity, and impunity

therefore, in this manner
did
My Son regale them

in His Regal Way

on to the
Crossroad of Jerusalem

so that along the way
with ears and eyes
they might
hear and see His
mighty wonders, words
deeds, & signs
Glorious

to behold:

# Upon Leaving Galilee

**on His trail**

they followed on

in full force
the pharisees, sadducees,
maccabees, and
those ever-presently wanting-

to-be's in

all their real and
imagined regal splendor out

-numbering the poor
Galileans
destitute, desperate

for a glimpse of
My Son, an echo of
His Voice, a

touch from Him,
even of His hem

but close-ringed they
My Son, the
lawyers, scribes, and high priests

hanger's-on every one
for some little jot or tittle left un-
crossed, un
-dotted or undone, even just one
of their six-hundred and 13
loopholed laws

so stopped He, mid-way
to the next village, out of
Caeserea Philippi

to gaze
at the vast array
before Him
and therefore to say

: be ye therefore

  wise as serpents, or
  gentle as doves?

  slow to anger,
  or swift to forgive?

  perchance, even more:  able
    in heart, or
    more feeble in mind?

and paused He,
in mid-speech
as in mid-tread; then

He resumed His pace

for yet a little while til
at a crossroad He

once again paused,
allowed the dust
to settle, to so be it

as He gazed

from east to west
south to north;
then spied a child who'd
at arm's length
slipped in unseen to

nearly touch Him, so

He reached out; and
the child reached out
a scrofolus withered hand, fingers
all gnarled and rheumatoid, nails bereft,
knuckles bulbous, swollen;

it hesitated near his sleeve;
His eyes met hers,
His palm graced her brow,
she gasped, inhaling at His touch;

then He spoke

: a certain poor man
  knew of
  a certain rich man

  together knelt they on

  the Sabbath; one
  prayed for
  loaves of bread, on
  the morrow; one
  prayed for
  a plentiful harvest
  of grain

  at the end of the day; I say

  which one prayed
  aright and
  which one prayed
  for which

in the pause He released
His palm from
the child's brow, and

her restored
pristine hand released
her grasp

on the cuff of His sleeve
then they smiled
at one another;
and she still unseen slipped
through the crowd

while He required
of them

: what say ye?

  of Sabbath prayer
  and
  Sabbath deeds?

glancing at the waning sun
whose lengthening rays
met His azure eyes

while naught but silence
reached His ears

and theirs; that their
tongues should lie
in quietness; and thus to His stroll
He returned, in the evening air

when with pausing, once
more, as the
Sabbath dawn lay behind them, setting
when once it arose before
them; then

He spoke
this unto them

: so, be ye therefore

   slowly maddened, or
   swiftly gladdened?

   what says your law?
to wit
their opulent silence
remained while they re-
turned away, even

His closest followers be-
came mute, as if dumb
-founded, lost

in their thoughts; and
in mine, I'm

pondering, which of
their laws
prohibits answering

on the Sabbath

and how shall My Son in
flesh appearing, ever
heal such

an endemic outbreak of
acute affluenza

**on a stony path**

that they trod, on and
on, near on to for four hours now
or more

the disciples, and certain other
johnny-come-lately ne-er-do-'ells and
assorted want-to-be's straggled
behind My Son, eager only

for some respite, surcease from their toil

footsore for
a wider, easier, broader
more pleasant way, thus they
called out,

"Master,
  we faint, for shelter
  shade, and rest

  we beseech you, please, pause,
  tarry yet a while . . . "

and so he led them
onto a little hill, not far off
nearby, where
no green pastures lay

but could be seen there from afar;
so into their minds

instead described He this, saying
: a well appeared
  unto a man as in a
  dry and dusty
  desert land; thirsting

  he lurched, after it
  as if a mere mirage of a
  well
  he'll sore travel toward

only to find
verily a hole, with
some water in it, but without

a bucket, gourd, or even a
leathern cup;

he at the rim leaned and
long looked into the
dark watery air, for just a draught
of that far away wellspring so
near, two arms' lengths
but away;

yea, some seven cubits deep the
water lay
but three cubits of air

separated him from it there;

and with none nearby to call to
for help, or aid; thus with
no one close by must he rely upon
what ever his wit
could provide;

and what

was nearby, but a pile of rubble
loose stones, pebbles,
gravel, and an occasional

Rock

yet nowhere a container
to carry nor
to convey the life-living water
to his lips
except his two hands;
and his wit

as My Son paused, and
let His gaze surmise along the long
horizon line, and then them
in silent expectancy,
awaiting His further words, so

He began again
: the man of thirst surveyed
  his scene, with

   his mind, in it he planned his work; then
   worked he his plan

   one by one, and two by two
   selected he hands full
   of gravel, pebbles,
   and stones; and an occasional

   Rock

   to drop into the well, with care
   he created a Mosaic layer

   that neither blocked the source
   nor impeded the flow but

   raised the water's level, til he
   with bended elbows could
   scoop into his two hands mouth-

   fulls of the cool refreshment and
   the life-bearing liquid to
   his parched lips and reins; wherein

   he was fully satisfied.

and then He stood to regain the
stony path; where on
they all stood there too, once
again upon their now rested feet;

to them then He instructed
: gather ye but a single stone of
  small to middling size

   that with comfort fits
   upon your tongue, to suck upon
   and draw from within that stone
   all the moisture in
   the world

until sated; from your mouth
you sometime later

let it roll away,

and ye shall thirst no more

then again they began their journey onto
Jerusalem, with His Face a-
glow from the rays of
the setting sun;

and each of them then with Him
alone in his own thoughts
of how now

to slake his thirst within

**near to the Sea**

of Galilee, not far from
Capernaum
alongside the shoreline
in line
more or less

His faithful followers
and

those others fatefull tended to
My Son, toward
Him they attended to

hear what He had to say
and how; thus,

: whyfore do those
 men there

 so mend their nets?

to which the fishermen
among them
there, James & John, and
Simon Peter & Andrew

looked askance
between themselves, and at
each other;

but His gaze
He kept steadfast upon
the fishermen, laps covered and
layered in nets, fingers
plying their trade

holes to fulfill;

so My Son carried on
: surely you know
 'why';

but for what 'end'
is it that
they do sew?

is it more praiseworthy
to catch;
or is it moreso

just to mend?

and then
they so seemed
to latch onto
their Master's meaning

save for the lawyers
scribes, and chief priests
as always
in attendance, schooling
about My Son who

shook their heads, wagged
their tongues, and
crossed and un-
crossed
their little jots &, their littler
tittles, & all their littlest
laws and loopholes

as ever they so appeared

moreover more intent to
amend Him, than
to listen to
Him

and His Story

**in a grove, or**

a glen, or a
glade

in the nearby shade
of trees cool
and soothing in the

early morning sun

My Son
took pause to say

: take heed
　of the Tree

　for truly it has
　truth to lend thee
　he, who has eyes to
　see with;

　marvel at its
　branches, that boast not
　neither the trunk
　nor the leaves

　nay, never should the
　fruit bare

　false witness to their

　mighty accomplishments; for
　they know

　without the root
　where hangs the fruit

　it so depends upon
　the leaves, the branches,
　and the trunk to all
　be sup-
　planted by

and so saying, He
withdrew within the bower, off
a little by Himself
to pray

and they, left behind
murmured over
their Master's Words

while I pondered then upon
what the limbs
of the Root of Jesse would

They yield

**that I mayest not**

seek neither my mother
nor my father

was I taken and given

to the Temple of the Lord
that one day I might
be
the Temple of the Lord
for all eternity

Love's pure Light

which flooded my mind
with Brightness

as My Son illumined
all our minds
in the noonday sun there

among the Galileans, some
Samarians, and
His usual
followers, hangers-on, and
detractors, to say

: from where comes
   the oil
    for your lamps

to all, He intended for
they who gathered there,
but not one so much
as stirred even
once in the Brilliance of
the rays

casting no shadows
among them;
no, not even the usual
Pharisee, and
his unusual followers

dared look unto Him
and upon His way, but
chose to study their toes,
a bare ripple
across their sandals;

but patiently, He
awaited
their reply; but there came none

still; so

they all awaited, as if
a cloud
to block the light
glaring upon them there;

and yet, no word
from Him, either; save,

His smile
ever there, Radiant Beams
for

His followers to bask in

and
walk in
along their pathway,
while I surmised
His intent

which put me in the mind,
again
of my tender, yonder years
when at three

I was summoned
among the unsullied others,
daughters of the Hebrews

who trimmed their lamps toward
me, at the Temple with the Dawn of

Redeeming Grace

that I might not stray
and
that I might captivated be;

and the priest
his hand upon my head
pronounced,

"The Lord has blessed
your name
among all generations

and because of you
the Lord will manifest
his redemption of
you, till the end
of days
among the children
and
the children's children
of all Israel."

and he placed
me

upon the third step

of the altar,
and I danced with
my feet
in the light, led by It

and the whole house
of Israel
poured forth in love;

and when from my reverie I
returned
to feel My Son's azure eyes

gently upon me

warming me
illuminating me, as I
heard Him say,

so enlightened

: let the Lord
  be a lamp
  unto thy feet
  and a
  light unto thy path

but at that

the elders, high priests scribes,
lawyers, & Pharisees only did they
shake their heads, and

not just once,
at this His nonce

# WHEN IN SAMARIA

**not far past the border**

inbetween Galilee and Samaria
nearer on to En-Gannim

My Son was asked, "And yet, Master,
  we proceed, unabated toward and, . . .
  and through . . . *into* . . . "

: yes, Peter?

"Master, most like us go a-*round,* about
  the united states of
  samaria; and yet
  we . . . we . . . "

as ever the Soul of Patience, after
Peter's hanging
pause, dangled awhile He had so let it
My Son replied, in kind
: yes, Peter; yes

"Master, -- I know how it is we save
  three days' travel, rather than
  six long days,
  by not going through, . . .
  and . . . but, Master,
  cutting a-

  cross,—through
  straight on to Jerusalem, for
  the Passover, . . . but,
  Master . . . the danger . . . "

: O, Peter, 'tis not the time saved,
  but the lessons learned

so He said, with looks of longing
when My Son saw
John, the belovéd, and me

arm in arm

walking along, as often
alone, the two

of us, yet
near among the very last of
His truest followers;

thus, He
surveyed them there, every one,
in his place, uncertain, and
unsure;
and so to ease them, He included them

: help me, yea, listen a while
  first, to this

then He began to say to
them this story,

　: a certain man went up
　from Galilee unto Jerusalem, but
　travelled he through
　Samaria instead; this certain man

　of wealth, manners, and prestige
　journeyed, as if from some yon distant
　land, traversing far from home
　through this country
　long despised, and reviled;

　it was also a land long despoiled;
　of evil will, and mal-
　contents intent
　upon wretchedness, to those

　whom they with their ill will did oppress,
　along the way, simple travelers
　like this certain man did they long
　to so transgress; therefore

　similarly, must he pass through the land

　as if across a field sown with
　devils' teeth and
　leprous scales flung from their tales

then He paused, all of His
onlookers and listeners
to once more survey;
until His gaze came to rest

upon Andrew, brother of Simon Peter; and
waited, til his eyes met his

: Andrew, continue our story; what
  do you say, of journeying through this heart-
  less land?  say so,

  how would you picture this dyspoiled
  place?

"Master,—me?"

: yea, Andrew, you have been
  a listener fine and rare; often have I
  heard you retell
  some of these my self-same stories;

  verily even some of the hardest
  with truth and honesty, so

  what say you
  to finishing thus my story?

caught unawares but not
unaware of his brother's eyes
upon him, and

their narrowing, which he seemed
to patently ignore; so, Andrew
answered My Son, always aware
and
always aware of all

: I know you full well, Andrew;
  so I pray you, continue, for me, in the
  manner I have begun, for you

"But, . . . me, Master, -- I . . . "

: yes, Andrew
  you; please, tell us

  what you know
  of this place we enter; of
  this land,
  and these people

  all of what you know;

  howsoever you will, Andrew

" I—similar unto thee, Master?"

: yes, howsoever thou will, Andrew;
  please

so Andrew began
in like manner after
My Son,

"They say, this land is
  most alike unto

  one despised, and most foul …
  in most disrepute, ever since
  the Assyrian kings asserted their

  torched-earth policy, and rule; and so they
  re-settled the land with

  the deported dregs of conquered
  peoples, to meld into
  one people bereft of heritage and
  common bonds; so that,

  they who were ravaged, ravage on;

at which
Andrew paused and chanced
a timid glance at
My Son

Who smiled and nodded, with one
eyebrow raised just enough

in encouragement; so
he continued forth, Andrew
even emboldened some

"And so,
  this certain man of wealth, he
  along the way that he
  walked alongside, passed by, himself
  next to a sty of wretched rancor,"

to pause, again, perhaps
gauging his metaphor's effect
and
glancing aside at My Son
Who slipped him His subtle smile

"Then, that said man, came unto
  a stile across a wicked way;
  toward a path beneath
  a bramble of bitter
  thorny réfuse, beyond which lay
  a trough of de-lousing swill,
  next to a bog brimming
  with wicked filth; nearby

  a trail of travail;

  mired in evil swill, beside a
  dunghill, ashy, fungus-flecked, with
  sore many flies worrying over it;"

when he paused again
as if only to catch his breath
his furtive eyes chanced an-
other glance
toward his Lord and
Master

Who further encouraged him with
: say on, Andrew; press on

to wit he eagerly
resumed,
"Near there, stood a puddle of
  putrid slag and slime,
  beside a trench of bile vile;

emptying too into
a fetid grimey latrine of offal so
overflowing into . . .

. . . into a pit of pity—no,
a . . . pit of piti-—
into a *pathetic* pit of
pity—so
surrounded, . . . so—"

Peter no longer able to
restrain himself, or it seemed,
face flushed, "No!" he interrupted him,
"A *petty* pit of pity!"

to which, all were silent;
save, My Son

: ah; well said, Peter

who basked in
the momentary ray of
Light, only to hear

: say on, Andrew;
  what else see ye there?

"A, . . . a stagnant pool
 of wretched excess, besmirched
 with rancid pus, and
 so foul defiled, soaked in
 slakeless sin; and . . .

and . . . and at last *at* his destination
that certain man procured, or
procured he, . . . a . . . a pure white
lamb, from . . .

where he retraced his
entire journey through the slough;

wherethrough the lamb led by his lead

whose ermine sides 'twere then
sullied and be-
deviled from the loathsome
sleaze of that foulsome land;

til at the border
that certain man of wealth

there was demanded of him
for safe passage from
one land unto the next that
that certain man must

let the lamb be slain;

forsooth that certain man must
have to relent; even unto
it being served, in part
and parcel, incarnadine, everso

rare

unto those very denizens so
that what was once
thick, opaque, and dull
could become

crystal clear, ever bright;
and whole."

afterwhich such a hush
fell among all
gathered there; and
with such expectant looks

all turned unto My Son

for what He would say
unto Andrew, still

catching his breath
and in wonder
and awe

at what such wonders his lips bespoke;

and to the still breathless
and speechless
Andrew, My Son

laid a gentle hand
upon his shoulder all aquiver,
: Andrew
  you spoke
  with such an inspired tongue;

  therefore your voice
  carried It afar;

  you have taken The Word, Andrew
  as your own, and
  rightly so;
  and have justly
  revealed your vision from

  the Lord your God;

  praise be, for yours too
  is a hard saying,

  to be sure

and naught among the
gathered did aver nor dare reply;
perhaps, could not

so stunned were they by
Andrew's awful tale

least of whom 'twas Peter,

still aslant in his looks
at his brother;

and the pharisees,
sadducees, doctors of
the law; the lawyers, scribes,
and chief priests

shook their grey and hoary heads
at what his words had wrought;

but again, to Andrew, spoke
My Son, only to him
however loud enough that
all those gathered round might
hear Him

: yea, indeed
  for what you have shared
  has been shown of

  the Lord your God

  as 'twas
  thusly shown unto
  the prophets and
  by them;

to then smile His smile

at the doctors of
the law, and
their scribes; and all of
the chief priests there around;

then My Son
as if to clear the clouded-over air
He pronounced

to all the throng
: what say you
  of the stories you
  have but heard and
  just seen

to wit, a lone
self-rightwise white-
headed doctor of the law
cautioned to speak forth, thusly

"O, Rabboni, there hast
  been but one parable
  spoken forth today;

why say ye
'stories,' as though there had
been two, or moreso told?"

: say you so, learnéd doctor

of the law;
two stories *have*
verily been before all of thee

unfolded;

one you have heard;
the other

you did but need to see

if,
you have the eyes with which

to see

and at his last word, did an ever-
so long pause ensue; and
into that extended silence His eyes
came to rest

on Peter, whose own eyes
furtively searched elsewhere; any-
where but My Son's

then, last of all
He turned and winked

at John

**in Samaria**

of all places, and
always
all the questions

"Who are my neighbors?"
"Wherefore they?"
"Whyfore we?"

and My Son's reply,
a smile
always; as if they

are children; and they

are with Him, in the shade where
He sat; they are
clustered around Him
so Heliocentric;
He sat, at

the center of them and
of their then known universe

Andrew & Simon Peter; and
James & John ever
-sidling closer to
His side

and so, again, arose

the Neighbor Question

to wit
He patiently replied

: one day
  a certain mother
  answered the knock
  at her door, shaped
  not a little unlike a heart

  the knock came again;
  and the mother
  opened her door to

her neighbor: she who'd
profaned her name

alack, and, alas, again
and again and
again,

but the neighbor's hearth had
fallen dark,
cold, and in ashes lay

and two appeals to two
other neighbors
who knew better this
neighbor's bitter tongue

their doors they had not yielded;

but this certain mother
gave forth from

her heart, and her hearth

a portion of her fire;
in the pot
she with tongs, placed
coals, alive and glowing

into this pot
that her neighbor might
carry home upon her

head, coals of fire
heaped therein

as was the custom to
carry there:
to her life

and also to her hearth
were then lit
and her home became warm
and lighted; so

self-satisfied she lived

then My Son stopped
to smile upon them all
gathered there

and He let His gaze come
to rest upon
the lawyers, scribes, elders
high priests, & pharisees
in their usual cluster

those who so often posed
the questions;

and then from them
came another

a Pharisee, uncrossed
his arms to ask,
"Teacher, what of
  the woman
  who lent unto her 'neighbor'
  new light from
  her hearth?"

My Son so answered
his question with
His own question, thus

: what say you to this,

  should we consider more
  how we are judged

  by our words
  or by our deeds?

and then in their prolonged
silence pronounced
was no mirth, nay, neither
any smirk

for well they knew

and so He decided
then their question He to
answer in full

: yea, the certain mother
  lived her life
  caring not; and
  fearing not

  what will the neighbors think

or say; as
I recall
My Son's words
left them speechless
in their geocentric clusters

for naught were their ears so
not unstopped; and
their eyes blinked, unseeing
as still their hearts beat

at the same rate

**not all women**

in Samaria
nearer to Gennai

are pure,
virginal, even as

in the beginning

when they are
conceived
to be

as at My Son's

speaking of the parable of
the wastrel daughter

when He
and His followers
paused
as ever, always, adjacent to

the market square
among
the publicans and sinners
and the pharisees;

and also there, a scribe and
lawyer of the
scriptures, albeit only of

the Decalogue;

and together they posed,
over those others also murmuring,
"Master,
 how ought we
 to bear the Law of Moses

 whence not to commit
 adultery

whenever it's been
priorly
committed, yea even multiple
adulterous acts,
as in one

like unto her,"
finger-pointing, per usual

at some poor barren soul
pitiful while pity less
cowering, hidden in the

shadows of
a corniced wall, hanging back
beneath the clouded sky, but
peering out
at the crowd around

My Son, so

at ease in
the hotbed of their hatred, as

ever; He looked from her
to them, to then
say

: a certain man
 and his wife
 had three daughters

 of whom
 the middle, saith

 "Father, I desire
 my portion
 of your goods be-
 quest to me

 with the giving
 of my hand,

 for I have been wooed
 and would be wed."

then he
and his wife
released unto her
the portion of dowry
allowed unto her;

afterwhich she journeyed
into a far off country
and was wed
to some man; but
in that far country she
was not
his first nor his second
wife; and when

he had spent all
she had to give; and
when

he had tired of her

he sold the middle daughter
to another man
in a country farther off;

that man too in time
tired of her, and
so sold her unto still

another man who put her out
to hire as an harlot;

later she was sold
again, into more sordid harlotry,

and woe, but the middle daughter
would have
filled her belly with

the crumbs of a humble pie

fallen
onto the floor off of
her father's table.

However, one day
sojourning in that same
far off and away country
a steward of
the middle daughter's father

happened to pass through the town
where she served as

an harlot for her fourth

husband; verily so,
even through her grim visage

the steward did
recognize the middle daughter, and
inquired of her master

howso could she be let,
or bought;

her cruel and
task-driven master replied,
"To me she is most dear,"
but the steward
answered, "My Lord
 would greatly desire her;

 what is the price?"

and when he was told so very much,
the steward
made haste, straightaway to
the father; upon hearing

the joyous but saddening news

he and his wife
enjoined the steward to
speedily return and

ransom their daughter;

to wit,
he did with immediacy.

Then the middle daughter
arose
and in the care of
the loyal steward did
journey forth to her
father, and to
his wife.

But when she was yet
a great way off
her father saw her,
and had compassion,
and ran to her; and fell
upon her neck;

and, lo, embraced her to
his bosom,
and kissed her brow.

and likewise did his wife.

And the middle daughter
said unto them,
"Father, Mother,

  I have sinned against heaven,

  and in thy sight; and am
  no more worthy
  to be called
  thy daughter"; but lo,
the father said to his servants,

"Bring forth the
  best gown, and put it
  on her;

  put rings on her fingers,

  and slippers on her feet:

  and in her hair
  a garland of roses,

bring to us
the fattened lamb,
and kill it;

and let us eat, and
let us be most merry;

for this my daughter
was dead, and is

alive again;

she was lost, and
is found;

she once was a slave
and is now set free."

And they began
to be full of merriment.

Now the eldest daughter
was returning from
the well; and
the youngest from
the market; and as they

came and drew near to
their father's house

where they heard music,

and they saw dancing and much,
much merriment. Then they
called out to one
of the servants, and asked

what these things meant.

And he said unto them,
"Your sister is come home;

and your father
killed the fattened lamb,
for he has

received her safe and secure;

because he has
bought her
with a great price."

But they were so angry;

and would not enter in:
so their father, and
their mother

came out to them, and
entreated them.

And, lo, they would not;
but answering
said to their father,

"O, these many years
have we both served you,

neither transgressed we
at any time
your least commandment
or bidding; nor

married any against your will,

but lean wholly
upon you, father,

and yet you never gave
us
a kid or a lamb,

that we might make merry
with our friends:

but as soon as
your wanton daughter
comes home, who

has sinned in her riotous living

with many foreign men,
and has been
a harlot to numbers more

you killed for her the
fattened lamb."

Then their father said
to them both, clasping both
their hands in his,

"O, Daughters,
you are ever with me,
and
all that I have is yours;

it is only right that I
and your mother
should make merry,
and be gladdened:

for your sister
was dead
and is alive again;

and was lost, and
is found;
she once was bound.

But now is free."

And when My Son had finished
thus saying, He
let His gaze find hers

no longer in the
cornered shade, for
the clouds had passed, the sun
its course
had run some and left her
in the half-dark where
the walls met so that

when His eyes
met hers
beneath her shawl,

'twas therein a twinkle.

while I
among the throng
could feel the press of their
bodies, and
the ebb and flow

of the day's malaise
so fraught
with their smug self
-assurance known, only

to the righteous, the elite, and
the morally superior

yet sensed there I
an ease
a release, as He

turned about

in their midst, and in
their minds; as

I pondered
howso at

the end
could one thus be
ever pure, all ways, always

virginal

even eternal
when at last, truly

it is finished.

**on the Sunday before**

the Sunday
before
His Resurrection

My Son as at Sabbath sat
at table at
the home of the

Pharisee of pharisees

so that
they might watch Him
all the more closely;
and that

all men might see he
does eat with
sinners

tax collectors, prostitutes, & publi-

cans; outsiders
of His Kingdom Come
His Will
to be done

but the meal is
a trap

not at which one's
to eat
but at which One's
to be eaten; alive

thus, My Son walks into it

their hospitality, and his, the
Pharisee's, a sham
where food and drink in
abundance, lies

in wait

He is
as a lamb
about to be
led to a slaughter, where
there's laughter
to be;

so My Son
smiles His smile, His
azure eyes, a-
twinkle
as if the waves sunlit on
the Sea of Galilee

at sunset reflect not
the light but
Is the Light

enrobed in eternal
patience My Son
at ease,
then there to please
reclines, and

awaits their
questionings, and
the Pharisee begins,

"O, teacher, why
 dost thou
 so often speak

 of children?"

: of whom
  would ye have me
  speak
"Why we here are
 all men, grown, and
 women, too,
 come of age; so

 speakest thou,
 to us."

to which He curled
His feet beneath His robe
spread out upon the foot of
the couch and
leaned
upon His elbow,
wistful

: would you not be
  children, again, if

  you could?

"Nay, master, we would
  be fraught
  to regress, to
  forego our learnéd ways.

  Whyfore?"

to gaze beyond their heads
: and yet, perchance
  would you rather be called

  childish, or
  child-like

but exhaling with impatience.
"Rabboni,

  we would be
  neither; we have
  surpassed such thinking,
  and being."

: suppose therefore
  in a certain country
  not so far off,
  away from where we are

  children play;
  and are so
  at play

  that when they are
  called

to sup, for the
evening hour hath
drawn nigh;

but they who are thus playing
fail to hear

and come not to the table;

what think ye then
of them?

child-like or childish

"Teacher,

of what import
be these stories.

We tire of such teaching.

The dinner hour
is at hand;
there are no children
here.
We partake."

and he clapped his hands
to bring forth the meal
and servants so appeared

with it, wherewithal all

did imbibe, and forthwith did
partake; save

My Son
Whose smile, faded
in the waning evening
twilit light of
passing day
and He did look

out of doors, through the door

at its leaving;
I see Him then, still

and am reminded of Him,
put in mind of Him

else
-wise, ineffable when

surrounded by
the sun, a golden rain-
bow; and a
halo

so free of sin, and
stain, the *macula*
original, not temporal, nor
eventual but eternal

when He

My Son's arisen,
awash in
Maternalism

**with nare a Samaritan**

behind us, and before us (about
  to beset us) and
Jerusalem clearly

in sight, to offer insight
by, My Son

paused,

a mere stone's throw from the
southernmost border be
-tween Samaria and Jerusalem

poised

to enter in, He interposed
by the side of the road
their Master
set about
to clue them in on the
coming disaster

of the Kingdom come
that His will be

done; so He set
them and they, a
little apart

that they might better
see and hear

Him from, His *Sacre Couer*

with the way to Jericho
lying in wait
before Him, and them

He then gathered them in, those
in attendance upon Him
round about

so circumscribed, they

the scribes, lawyers, pharisees
and saducees; disciples
brigands, hangers-on, the ne'er-
do-wells, the doubters and
the pouters, Simon Peter, Andrew
James & John . . . and all

the other Zebedee wanna-be's; the
doctors of
the law; the poor, the
needy; the possessed and the

dis-possessed, and the dys-possessed

and still others, ill and
especially of ill will (wondering,

  so aloud
  in their heart of hearts if

  this teller of
  parabolic tales
  would be wanted to

  reign over them); thus,

that one and all be awakened
in their ears and opened
in their eyes

to the blaring Light

of His eyes and voice,
as He began

  : and there were the three
    called before
    their master; and therefore
    before him

    bowed they down,
    for any his least bidding

then he gave them
according to his delight
talents
of gold, silver, and brass,

and of precious stones

to the first he gave
in number
12, all in all
3 of each;

to the second
gave only 3 each of
gold and silver and brass;
and to the third

he gave to him
half gold and half of
precious stones

both in threes;

the first two
bowed and thought
evreso highly of their master for

what they each had been given;

but the last, the third
walked away
head down,

grumbling, and murmuring

fraught in mind o'er
only

what he'd not been given

like unto their earthly visions of
treasures in heaven, glittering

and clinking, tinkling, their

reward, pieces of silver
gold, brass, and precious stones

given or gotten

cared they before their Master
Who answered
before they replied, aloud
or otherwise, that
: then the master, when

   he had their talents thus bestowed

   lingered not, that they might
   wait upon him
   but instead left them, there;

   so, thus will it be

furthermore, so said My Son
: that 'tis when
   the Kingdom of God Is
   nigh, at hand

   immediate in Immancence

   so too, as when those three last
   saw their master, who had

   said unto them, 'Lo, but those
    mine enemies, which would not

   that I should reign over them,

    bring hither
    and slay them before me,
    at my return.'

   and whence comes, you may say
   such a passage?

so speaking; then He paused, a while
to smile His smile
at their supposéd blind and deaf and
dumbed-down guile

as if a cloak upon their hearts
left them

ill-concealed, and not revealed

as surrounded by their shifting
and shifty glances a-
round the crowd
I perceived in
those their sidelong looks an
out-of-the-corner wish
for justice

when what they should
want, and long for

is Mercy

so thought I then; when James and
John . . . and Andrew; and . . .
Simon Peter . . .
stood rapt amongst them there, before

Him, and the steep steps

about to lead them
on their way, and His, to journey to

Jerusalem, and to the Mount
along the Ascent
of the Psalms, from the heart

of David, . . . to My Son of David's

# So Nearing Jerusalem

**and so**

in the town ahead, Bethabara,
lived
a certain Centurion

by the Order of Rome, *S.P.Q.R.*

My Son, paused
in the road, thereon

to let the dust of the earth
settle among them there,
on their feet, in their hair, upon their
cloaks; and staffs,
to say

: what of this man
  paid to uphold
  the *Pax Romana,*
  nothing more

  what of he, trained
  to fight
  and slay the enemy, little
  else

  but rarely stirs he abed
  afore the hour
  of noon

  and long stays he awake, through
  the late night watch nigh in-
  to the morning

  yet never once
  in many a year, not any one
  of those in this town

  has ever seen him
  draw his sword, and even so

  faith fully each
  *annum*
  draws his entire and total
  pay

to which, He paused
again; then looking, round about
Him

they then resumed their Way

until
that day to cancel a
debt, *in totum*

in the City of David, ahead
Jerusalem

according to Thy Word;
there upon a New Standard, He
would bear,
thus, it will be inscribed

*I.N.R.I.*

and so ever fitting for Him, My Son
to be, He
<u>the</u> *Procer Pax*

**: and who**

  are our enemies

began My Son with
such dread
words, a

sword, a

-likened in my heart
up to the hilt

whereon's inscribed
Simeon's initials and a
-dorned with the
family crest

a pair of triangles, a
-ligned as if crossed-o'er
Venn diagrams, My
Son's heart and
mine, once One; now a

-cross
this gathered crowd
about Him; they beat

in unison, mine here
His there

whensoforth He adjures
in no mere jeremiad
tones, them to hear
the Truth
as

: not to be confused
  when our friends
  stand so near, so close, and a
  -round
  even at our back

  especially when
  there's nowhere else
  to turn, alike

when once a certain man
called out to

friends, neighbors, and
countryfolk to
hearken unto,
"what I have heard
 our lord say

what he does expect that

we, among
ourselves must
decide upon

our being, well

that others, without us
may know

that we are one;

you in me, I in you,
we in each other; and that

he our lord, over
-all is, over all Is; one, with many

members, and all
members one; re-
members he, for

plenty there be, within us

willing to
forsake or over
-rule our
oneness, for their

singularity must be
more than our plurality
less; unless

we be unifed," so
did he say, such a man as
he, one
alone, a
lone one, a
-1-

   one; therefore, that was
what a certain man
said unto his
brethren

and so He concluded,
My Son
all to them closely
gathered there, in their
collective silence, an enclave
hushed in
wonderment at this
another of His not

so easy sayings, a
-cross the distance a
-tween us; in the
crowd of His

'friends'

that would come
to ever
draw us apart;

but will ever closer
be drawn
until at that Friday eve

when He was again placed
in my lap

to cuddle, Our last
Last Embrace a
-ligns, perfectly His Heart
with mine; and

the beat, again
IS One, only
mine, this time; for
-ever posed in Our *Pieta,*

the Pity of Eternity

**on Mount Olivet**

a Sabbath day's journey
away from Jerusalem

My Son sat

not yet swept up
in the tide
of time
upon someone neither waits

nor out-
waits; save, My Son
from there surveys
the gathered throng

to say
: and it came to pass
　one day
　a certain landowner
　with plots

　of land in many lands

　said unto
　his one and only son,
　"Go forth
　　into my most distant
　　landholds
　　and collect those rents

　　most held longest
　　in arrears"

　to wit, his son replied
　"I go, father,
　　whithersoever and
　　wheresoever thou willest"

　and he did;
　but among those tenants
　farthest removed
　the son found

some in gross arrears

from famine, bad
management, ill-use, and
neglect; others just

from indolence, and insolence;

and yet, by his accounts
some he forgave, or
cancelled, many he re-
duced, and others collected
fair—while a few

who could afford so,
he increased, even one a
treblefold;

but among them and from
nearly all, in debt
an outcry to the heavens

arose; they bewailed: this son even on
his father's supposéd behalf has
been unfair, and hath

levied judgment and mercy

unevenly, yea, at
his whim has he decided

who and how
each should repay, or not.

and so,
they murdered him

the son of the father;

but then
they cowered in fear
that for their deeds he in
his retribution might
destroy them, and

   their children
   and their children's
   children

   like the chaff
   which the wind
   driveth away;

   but to this day
   it has not happened;

   yet

then He smiled upon them there
they who thought
to receive

but another sermon, from
this mount, too; or
at least some

barley loaves and fishes

for their want

but not a stone, nor a
serpent,
as they then some
among them

thought upon it

**those who glean**

in threes
most poverty-stricken
are, as

when My Son a field
of grain
passed by, with His disciples a
-longside the side of

the road
to Jericho, near to that field
He paused

to see, and say

: those three women there
  stooped, bent over with care are
  for their children's sake
  and
  for all the world

  the poorest of the poor

  therefore 'tis
  no one poorer than
  they who have
  no bread

again, the pause
as ever

for the ears and
the eyes, to awaken
and open

that the heart might remember
and in rhythm
recall: Ruth
longsuffering, and patient
in the field of Boaz to
glean and gather after the reapers
there among his sheaves

she, who too, and first

found favor in her
lord's sight,
that she might be

all our forebearance

in her downcast look; for how much
more her mere morsel of
parched corn,
when dipped in vinegar in

her not yet sorrow for
those yet, meant

to be,

too with Him, My Son;
Who said

: for bread have they those three
  none,
  but would
  for the sake of their children

  rustle among the plucked
  husks; lo, nor picked
  up not they three any
  pebbles, stones, nay even a grain
  of sand, nor
  gravel

  that no sediment be made
  to bread,
  save though through a

  Rock,

  crushed and
  bowed down, for all

  Isracl's sake

so My Son said, for-
evermore
: whoso asks for bread
   in the night

   of a friend?

and It came then to me
to know, My Son

'twill not He be
restored by
the dawn's earliest of
Early Light,

to rise
not like the sun,
but as the Son;

and May yet then again

**after the Procession**

after the Triumphal Entry into
the Holy City
on a colt but of a foal

My Son

after a turn about in
Jerusalem

walked on Monday of
Holy Week
with His disciples, fol-
lowers, new-found
adherents, speculators, hangers-
on, doubters, nay-sayers, and

pit-diggers, snare-setters, &
trap-layers, all among the

usual unusual curiosity seekers

to the Zion Gate
nearest to the crest of Mount Zion

and as was His
custom
to pause, He did

before
the Cenacle, purported
to be
His forebear's pseudo-tomb

so saying, began He
: the man who tastes wines
  and is a steward of
  the vine,
  for a living
  he lives
  to taste, and see;

  he tests
  them

with his tongue, and
gums, and
his lips
they assist him

even his teeth serve
him, and his purpose, to
strain, and
to swish through

the fruit of the vine,
once water,
not yet blood, or vin
-egar [as an aside,
  with His casual smile] then

wine again

for good, and
for once and
for all

to pronounce the steward states,
'the Good Wine hast
 been kept til now.'

then He sighed, looking at
no one in particular
except perhaps for a moment into
Nathan's eyes, not the least
of those His brethren there, thence

His gaze
came to rest upon that
same familiar line
of the horizon
but in His customary
pause
none dared inter
-rupt nor question Him
His silence

though their eyes
fast upon
His lips they openly gazed

so that He
full filled their
wonderment with
:  do not even the Gentiles
    say the same

but I pondered in my heart
howso on
the Thursday next He'd
come a second time
to this site and in
an Upper Room
partake of one last last-request meal, yea

even a pseudo-Supper,
where He'd pray

: let the words of
   My Mouth
   and
   the meditation of
   My Heart

   be acceptable
   in Thy Sight, O Lord

   My Strength,
   and
   My Redeemer

so that He mayest be
the Christ

the Chrism One

of me, and Thee;

when on that Maundy night the
Lineage of
the House of David has

come Home

# An Epilogue, In Kind

**and so, 'tis this Is**

the last
of My Son's lost
parables; composed

at the side of the
road, outside of an
inn, where upon the ground
He lay

His sweet head down

to better look
into the sky, the
Heavens above

looked down upon Him there

remembering His mount
to whereupon He'd enter into
Jerusalem through
the city's Golden Gate,

so then Self-composed, He

this
: and in the fields
  by night a
  lamb at peace so safely
  lay beside a ewe until the
  break of day

  when the flock
  restless
  left the pasture green
  and
  wandered about, me
  -andered, yea
  in a valley in shadows

  far flung from
  still waters

  til at length he and she
  separated to be

whence at a table
in the presence of
an enemy

the lamb's prepared,
dependents
to be restored;
and the ewe

awaits in want
of a shepherd's staff;

for
the lamb's
last remains, them

they have been cast upon
a dunghill

scattered with the remnants of
a late repast

next to a
husk of bread
and a
crushed and leaking wineskin

as of olde

and at His pause
those usuals
still gathered there were
sorely puzzled

but at that moment
there arrived
James & John, Peter & Andrew
with their Master's remembrances
again

for a meal
to come
in an upper room;

Who said then unto them

: Aye,
  My Time has come

**Additional Praise**

In the finest tradition of St. Benedict's *Lectio Divina*, Carl Winderl powerfully enters into Mary's own reflections on the Life and message of her beloved Son. *The Lost Parables of Jesus* is a poignant, touching, searing encounter with the Crucified Christ, with Love Incarnate. It was Jesus, after all, Who promised His disciples that He would send His Spirit to guide them into "all truth," and the deepest treasures of Scripture are often illuminated by the sort of *Lectio Divina* prayerful imaginative, reading of Scripture which St. Benedict, and his faithful servant, Carl Winderl, faithfully practice.
>—**Dr. Kenr R. Hill**, Senior Fellow and co-founder of the Religious Freedom Institute, Russian Historian, author of *The Soviet Union on the Brink*; former president of Eastern Nazarene College; Assistant Administrator of the U.S. Agency for International Development; and Senior Vice-President of World Vision. Hill came into full communion with the Catholic Church in 2013.

In *The Lost Parables of Jesus*, Carl Winderl offers an imaginative expansion of Jesus' teaching by storytelling during His last days, an expansion that includes the sharp perspective of His loving Mother.
>—**James Phelan**, Distinguished University Professor of English at the Ohio State University.

Don't just read this book. Absorb it. Let it seep into your heart like a healing oil. Notice the insights, the images, the what-ifs, the wordplay, the joy of Mary's account, as translated by Carl Winderl. See the Life of Jesus in a new way. Discover the parables that surround you. And magnify the Lord. Thank you, Carl, for this balm.
>—**Dean Nelson** is the founder and host of the annual Writer's Symposium By The Sea, and the journalism program at Point Loma Nazarene University. His next book, coming out in 2025 from Rowman & Littlefield, is *Talking to Writers*. His book *God Hides in Plain Sight* was published by Brazos Press in 2009.

One of my favorite poets has done more of the work that we have come to expect —writing lines that dig deeply into the history and story and power of the Holy Writ to shape our faith.
>—**Robert Benson**, author of more than twenty books on the spiritual life & named as a Living Spiritual Master by *Spirituality & Practice*.

Through Carl Winderl's *The Lost Parables of Jesus,* readers can delight in the mind-play necessary to understand the message of the Gospels in the way Jesus himself conveyed it—through parables. Though their tropes are drawn from biblical tradition (oil lamps, fruit of a vine, a prodigal daughter, mending nets, the poor man and the rich man, words vs. deeds), Winderl's parables are new, fresh stories that convey the spirit of Jesus's wisdom and love while adeptly engaging readers in the act of interpretation through masterful word-play and line breaks: Jesus's three foes are "duplicitous" even "triplicitous." Those who seem incurable of greed have "acute affluenza." On both the unity among believers and the dual meaning of faith as both "remembering" Jesus and re-membering the Church with His followers: "all / members one; re- / members he . . . ," and as Mary reminds us, all of her Son's stories are told with "a smile /always."
—**Mary Ann B. Miller**, founding editor, *Presence: A Journal of Catholic Poetry*; and professor of English, Caldwell University

Winderl strikes again. With *The Lost Parables of Jesus*, Voice is given to the quiet observers of the New Testament. The familiar is taken and examined from a different perspective, allowing the readers to step out of their comfort zones and expand their world view. The lyrical flow of the pieces takes the readers on a journey. Weaving words into visions, Winderl sweeps his readers along the path taken by Jesus and His disciples. Mary's insight grants passion and Life into the Gospels in an enriching manner that will allow the readers to step into each stop along the way.
—**Zachary Winderl**, author of the *Atom & Go* sci-fi western trilogy: *Genesis, Trinity,* and the forthcoming *Wastelands*. At "The Literary Busker" he can be followed for his occasional 'Writings and Musings' about literature and life. Also, he's the son of Carl Winderl.

## Author Bio

Christened in the Polish National Trinity Catholic Church and baptized in the Church of the Nazarene, **Carl Winderl** is the beneficiary of his grandmothers alternately ferrying him one Sunday to a Catholic mass and the next to a Protestant worship service. *The Lost Parables of Jesus* is a reflection of those combined influences over the years.

He earned a Ph. D. in Creative Writing from New York University and an M.A. in American Literature & Creative Writing from the University of Chicago.

Formerly, he was a Professor of Writing in the LIT/JRNLSM/WRIT/LANG Dept., at Point Loma Nazarene University in San Diego. Taking early retirement from PLNU in January, 2018, he embarked on a series of 2-year mission assignments in Zagreb, Croatia; Kyiv, Ukraine; and Przemysl & now Krakow, Poland, where he serves in a similar assignment.

Finishing Line has published four other collections of his Marian poetry: *Mary Speaks of Her Son* (2005), *la Via de la Croce* (2008), *Behold the Lamb* (2015), and *The Gospel According . . . to Mary* (2021).

In addition, his Marian poetry has been linked with Thomas Merton, Pier Paolo Pasolini, John Donne, *et al.* at—https://udayton.edu/imri/mary/p/poems-by-carl-winderl.php—under the auspices of the International Marian Recearch Center & Library, hosted by the University of Dayton, where his Rosary sequence of twenty poems can be found under the title of *Les Mysteres*.

www.ingramcontent.com/pod-product-compliance
Lightning Source LLC
Chambersburg PA
CBHW020337170426
43200CB00006B/419